Don't Let the Church Steal Your Family

Don't Let the Church Steal Your Family

Yolanda Gilliam

To order additional copies of this book, contact:
Xlibris Corporation
1-888-795-4274
www.Xlibris.com
Orders@Xlibris.com
33962

Contents

ACKNOWLEDGEMENTS

To my Lord and Savior Jesus Christ, I thank you for using me as a vessel to do your will and work. Jesus you are my King and my everything. I dedicate myself and this book back to you.

To my mother & best friend Jane C. Hairston, I love and appreciate you. Thank you for keeping fire underneath me to finish this book. You are a true blessing to me. Love you much yo-yo.

To my son Michael whom I love dearly, thank you for encouraging mommy to finish this book. Besides Jesus, you are one of the reasons I enjoy living. I love you very much.

To my brothers' James, Carl & Joshua, I love you all very much. Thank you for believing in me.

To my sisters' Rita & Frances, I love you. Thank you for supporting me.

To my Aunt Lilly and cousins Jessica and Christina, I love and appreciate you. You are always there whenever I need you.

To my beloved Bishop and First Lady W.A. Garrett, words can't express my appreciation and love I have for you. Thank you for pushing me to go after my dreams and visions. This has been a dream come true. Love you much!

To my extended family and friends, thank you for your support and prayers. Love you!

INTRODUCTION

Whether you're working an 8 to 5 job, watching T.V. or even taking a hobby, you can overdo anything. As saints we must have a balance between our participation in church and the time we spend with our families. The essential element that makes the church is the family. Many saints believe the building is the church. People who have accepted Jesus Christ as their personal Savior makes the church. There are many distractions in the body of Christ which include position, clothing, function and more. Ask yourself, "Is there anything other than Jesus Christ that can save you or get you to heaven?" Is there some great formula? The answer is no. Why do we make salvation seem so difficult or a turn it into a twelve step program.

Which package have you purchased?

Package A

(10)	3x3	Come as you are and stay as you are portrait
(5)	5x7	Know the church language (Praise Him, Alleluia)
		(Classes are available at the **'Know the church lingo school'**)
(1)	8x10	How to spend less time with Jesus and more time at church

Package B

(15)	3x3	Stay as you are but have at least three characteristics of Christ
(7)	5x7	Includes free baptism and prophecy
(3)	8x10	Earn a position in the church while you and your spouse work out the details of your Godly divorce

Package C

(25)	3x3	Stay as you are but you must ignore at least three people every Sunday excluding bible study
(10)	5x 7	Includes a free baptism, Receive a newsletter entitled **'How to join the Church Click'** and read a bible scripture once a month (if that's to much read at least one scripture a year excluding holidays.)
(5)	8x10	Take a picture with the Pastor and First Lady as they pretend they like you and you like them. Also includes a fake I like you pose with your church enemies and PK kids (Pastor Kids)

Package D—Ultimate Package (Popular Package)

(50)	3x3	You get to ignore 20 people because you're a leader
(20)	5x7	The church click, Pastor and First Lady accepts you because you gave a generous offering.
(10)	8x10	You forsake your family for church activities, and what's great you have been nominated president of the world's renowned click (Yeah! You've finally learned how to be professionally and spiritually snotty)
(2)	11x17	The famous portrait—You get to take a pose with the saints who ran people out of the church because they didn't meet their expectations, Oh, I mean God's expectations. Congratulations!

All packages include that you accept Jesus as your Lord and Savior, free webpage with a picture of you and the church click, one free dinner and women must out dress the First Lady at least once a month.

Pathetic, you may say but the church has turned into a **big joke**. The unsaved don't take the church seriously. Our own Christian family seeks unsaved people and the psychic world for help instead of Jesus. What kind of example is this setting for unsaved people? Who really wants to be saved? Where are God's peculiar people?

The Lord gave me a vision of the saints and the demons. He showed me a large football field and the stands were loaded with demons. They were eating popcorn, drinking beer and holding up signs. The signs said, "Get em tiger", "Rip em apart", "Thata girl", and "You go boy". The opposing teams were the saints. The saints were on the football field fighting one another, calling each other out of their name, backbiting, lying, manipulating the pastor, families were divorcing, children were turning in their parents and there were a few saints praying in the corners of the fields. I was so disturbed by the dream I couldn't sleep for weeks. Can you imagine the devil doesn't have to work hard to destroy us anymore; we're doing a great job ourselves. The devil is encouraging the body of Christ to fight one another and keep up the good work.

The Devil doesn't have to work hard to destroy believers we are doing a good job destroying ourselves.

God help us through these troubled times!

I pray that this book will enlighten all pastors, leaders and saints to realize that this nonsense must stop NOW! We are allowing disharmony and discord to ruin our families and our church. Don't you think enough is enough?

Enjoy!

THE FAMILY

The Inspirational family appears to be the ideal family. They come to church together, spend quality time with one another and put God first. Let's meet them.

Bro. Inspiration

Praise Him!

I guess you've noticed by now my name is of biblical origin. I have been saved for a number of years. I'm the head and not the tail, my family follows me as I follow Christ. My family understands how important my position is and what it takes to run the church. I am a true leader I respect my elders; I treat my wife like a queen, my daughter like a princess and my son like a prince soon to take his throne. God has truly filled my quiver. My children are blessed going in and blessed going out. I'm not what I want to be but I'm getting there by the grace of God. My father taught me how to be a man of God, husband and a father. Now the same teaching flows to my beloved children. No one knows me like my family! Praise the Lord!

What an ideal Christian man. Now let's meet his beloved wife and children.

Mrs. Inspiration

Uh! I'm glad you finally got to my interview. That man ain't did nothing for me since we got married. Queen, yeah right! Why is this queen still in the same clothes from five years ago? Oh yeah, because he claims the money he

Yolanda Gilliam

makes is going towards the church and retirement. It looks like I'm retired. He said Queen, Uh; he hasn't taken me to go get a decent meal in ten years. Well, let me stop lying, he has taken me to Taco Bell recently. This man is such a fake. I go to church day after day, praying and fasting. Where has it got me . . . ? No where. I'm bitter, unloved and tired! My children don't know who I am, hec I had to look at my birth certificate just to remind me who I was and where I come from. This man hasn't kissed me in so long my lips are now permanently chapped and brittle. Queen alright! He makes me sick. Well anyway I want to invite you to come to my church, I may be messed up but that doesn't mean you will.

Amy Inspiration

My parents are weirdoes and they both have issues. Ever since I could remember my dad pretends everything is great and my mom is always trying to make him face reality. My parents don't act like they believe in God. They are so busy in their world they could care less about me. I have been trying different things to make me happy but it's only a temporary fix. You know what I mean right? Sex, a little weed, dancing, that kind of stuff but it doesn't last forever. I tried the Jesus thing but he takes too long to answer. Evangelist Lee said it took God too long to give her a husband so she went and found one for herself. She preached that message at youth night! Evangelist Lee is such a great example. I wish my family and I could eat dinner together, have family talks but that will probably never happen. Dad & Mom have bible bowl, counseling service, choir rehearsal and revivals. The chance of having quality time with my family is impossible. The only quality time I had with my mom was in the womb connected to the umbilical cord. Oh well, come to our youth services, no one knows what we do in our private lives, just be fake that's the only requirement.

Mavry Inspiration

Hey guys, my dad says I'm a prince. The last time I saw my dad open a car door for my mom was in front of the church folks five Sundays ago because it was treat your wife like a queen day at our church. Ever since my dad got promoted to the Deacon position he's been convincing mom to open the door for him. My dad is so insane. We never have those father and son talks. My mom always says I'll be just like my father because I have his genes. I guess I'll be like her, bitter, hurt and unloved. If you look at the whole picture I have both their genes and that's really scary. I try to pray but the T.V. is always interrupting me or my play station. I wish I could spend one day with my family at a park or restaurant. It's seems that ever since dad got the new position at church he hasn't been the same. I thought going to church, bible study, revivals, all day fast and prayer victuals were supposed to help change you. I guess it did change him a little, he finally said Hi son, and God is good when I was eating my breakfast. I literally cried because I hadn't heard anything from him in a long time. I know God sees my hurt and pain but it's really hard for me to believe right now. Well I gotta go catch a T.V. show called **'Crossing Over'** (The psychic channel). Maybe I can get some sort of answers for my problems.

THE ROLE OF THE FAMILY

In Ephesians 5:22-33; 6:1-3 it says:

Wives submit yourselves unto your own husbands, as unto the Lord. For the husband is the head of the wife, even as Christ is the head of the church: and he is the saviour of the body. Therefore as the church is subject unto Christ, so let wives be to their own husbands in everything. Husbands, love your wives even as Christ loved the church, and gave himself for it; That he might sanctify and cleanse it with the washing of water by the word, That he might present it to himself a glorious church, not having spot or wrinkle, or any such thing; but that it should be holy and without blemish. So ought men to love their wives as their own bodies. He that loveth his wife loveth himself. For no man ever yet hated his own flesh; but nourisheth and cherisheth it, even as the Lord the church: For we are members of his body, of his flesh, and of his bones. For this cause shall a man leave his father and mother, and shall be joined unto his wife, and they two shall be one flesh. This is a great mystery: but I speak concerning Christ and the church. Nevertheless let everyone of you in particular so love his wife even as himself and the wife see that she reverence her husband.

Children obey your parents in the Lord: for this is right. Honour thy father and mother, which is the first commandment with promise; That it may be well with thee, and thou mayest live long on the earth.

The role of the family has been negatively twisted by T.V., secular role models, and the church. As saints of God we must put the family back in first position. Please don't encourage or compromise your family for anyone or anything. Let's take a look at the vital roles a family must have in order to be successful.

THE MAN

The man's role of the family is to protect, teach by example, lead, be a visionary and maintain strength.

God designed man to protect his family from distractions that cause decay, corrosion and bacteria of the family. God takes the position of each family member very seriously. It is so important for men to take the time to love their wives in order for them to respond with a positive attitude. Showing love to your wife keeps balance and a flow of the Holy Spirit moving in the husband/wife relationship. God talks to the man and impregnates him with vision for his family and himself. (Women this is where you must keep your husband lifted up in prayer.) Every man must have a vision, write it down and execute it. Don't procrastinate. Procrastination will kill your vision and eventually your family.

Secondly, the man must teach by example. Men, your wife and children will respect your position highly when you put God first. It's important to have family bible studies, honor your wife and love your children by spending quality time with them. Find out what your wife likes and dislikes. Do the same for your children. Be attentive to the needs of your family so the devil won't have a place in your home. Have family chats and keep up with what's going on with your family's spiritual and physical needs.

Thirdly, men, never let another person take your place. For example, Grandma Ellie is always helping out with the children because you and your wife are working 10-15 hour shifts. The wife is frustrated with life and finds comfort in talking with Deacon Snake who has been waiting for the opportunity to minister to her every need. Your teenagers are constantly on the phone with friends from the other worlds luring them to do wrong. By the time you try to find quality time you have a revival, deacon meeting, Sunday school, Sunday service, bible study and counseling service. Oh yeah!! Etc., etc., etc.

Men take your position back from the devil that stole it away so easily. Don't believe that statement **'Women can do it all by themselves.'** That's a prideful lie. If God intended women to take on all the family responsibilities, there would be no need for the man. The family can't function without the husband or wife. The anointing flows from the man's head and down to his family.

You can't be complete without Jesus Christ. God wants you to know that he encourages family. He wants you to remember that you are not an island by yourself. You can only be complete by doing things the way God instructed you to do them through his word. Jesus said, **"I am the way, the truth and life. No man cometh unto the father but by me." (John 14:6)** You need your family and your family needs you. It's important to know who your family is in Christ and who you represent. Like my mom tells me to this day, you can't go wrong if you follow what Jesus says. We are looking for this super formula. I hate to break it to you but there's not one. God is simple and to the point. Obey and be blessed. Disobey and be cursed. Men your family should be a team of unity. Begin to act like you are a royal priest hood, a peculiar people. Focus on being God's kingdom builder.

Lastly, men become a visionary. A vision should be written down and executed. A vision is a dream or idea a person wants to see happen or come true. Your vision should be visually posted in a special place to review everyday. Your vision should be prayed and fasted over constantly. It should never be discussed with anyone other than the person whom God designates you to share it with. Negative words are powerful so don't let the bull dog vision breakers get a hold of the vision God gives you. Let's face it; everyone does not have our best interest at heart. Most of the time, people's intentions are not right. Because we want to be apart of the in crowd, we compromise by telling them our vision. Once the vision is shared with them, they become jealous, haters, and miserable because you are moving in the right direction. The vision is now under severe demonic attack. It takes longer for the vision to come to past because you shared it when it should have been kept to yourself. Let me give you some advice. BE QUIET! Never compromise your vision, salvation, family or self. Don't share the vision until it comes to past. The vision God gives to you, should never be taken lightly or shared without his permission. The vision holds the key to your future and breakthrough. So please SHHHH!!!

In conclusion, strength should be displayed by a powerful prayer life. Strength in the physical is fantastic but spiritual muscles are even better. A pastor once told me if prayer can't do it, it can not be done. Isn't that the truth? Without prayer we are super weak. Men should be the first ones on their knees and the last ones on their knees. Strength can only be gained through communion with the Holy Spirit. Have you ever tried to get a prayer accomplished while playing loud music? Wasn't it difficult? Could you hear God's voice? When you pray, get quiet before the Lord. Prayer gives you an opportunity to speak with the Lord and wait for him to respond back to you. Prayer is strength and power. This strength will carry you through a tough day, shine light in the midst of darkness, give you insight where there are clouds, tell your wife she is the most wonderful woman in your life which lifts her spirits out of a dry place, give your children the encouragement they need to face difficult obstacles and bring you to a higher calling with Christ.

If you are a man stop being a man and become a man of God. Be who God has called you to be. Lead, take charge and accept responsibility. (Quote from Pastor Jewel Jones) Know what you want out of life and you are sure to have miracles, breakthroughs and overflows. (Quote from Bishop W.A. Garrett) These are quotes from Men of God who have deposited valuable information from God's mouth and imparted them in my spirit. I praise God for true men of God in my life.

I'm glad God made men to be the head and not the tail. **Isn't it time you turned around and put your body back in the right position?**

THE WOMAN

The woman's role of the family is to love and assist her family through prayer.

Men are the ships and women steer them. Women need to be sensitive to the Holy Spirit when it comes to the family. The family depends on her support and nurturing.

Love

The bible says women should love their husbands as Christ loves the church. Because love is a powerful action word, women should display love as an honor. Whether good or bad times, love should be displayed in your family relationship.

Displaying such power, mends arguments in the house, brings the family closer together and sets the tone for forgiveness and overlooks offenses. Be the first to say I was wrong. Don't let negative actions reign in your household. Break the power of darkness by loving the hell out of the situation. A women's foundation should be founded on love. Some of the excuses I hear for the reasons it's hard to display love is: 'I was hurt a long time ago. I'm incapable of loving anyone.', 'It's too painful to forgive or love the person who did those horrible things to me.'

Let me tell you a story about someone who should have never forgiven people like us.

There was a man who came from heaven to die for a people who hated him. These people were selfish, ungrateful and deserved to die. This man was innocent but he chose death instead of life. He knew that through his death we had access to life everlasting. He let us beat, torture, curse and kill him. He never said a mumbling word. What kind of man would give his life for someone who deserved the penalty of death? No man, woman, boy or girl in history has ever experienced such a beating like this man. Do you know him? Have you tried him? If you have a sincere relationship with Jesus, how could you go against your brothers and sisters in Christ?

Why do we make so many excuses not to do right according to the word of God? Stop making excuses. Excuses will kill your destiny and eventually your family.

He loved us so much that despite our attitude, disposition and sin he died for everyone in this world. He not only proved his love by saying it but he proved it by what he did. The ultimate sacrifice he gave for us was his life. God is love.

Women, you may feel forgotten or overlooked by your family but one thing is certain, God sees everything you do, say, look at and hear. He is watching your every move. He is a rewarder of them that diligently seek him. Your family needs you. Without you there wouldn't be a family. Don't take your position lightly. Your love is needed. Your husband needs your praise. The children need your stroke of confidence, your church family needs your presence and most of all God needs you to create balance in the body of Christ. Women teach your children and those around you to love unselfishly. Be a true virtuous example of love displayed through your Christian walk with Christ.

There is no greater love than a man lay down his life for his friend.

Assisting through Prayer

Assisting is not an easy job but the rewards of it are indescribably joyous. Women of God need to be aware of what's going on around themselves and their family. When you're driving it's important to keep your eyes on the road because you might get lost or even get hurt. A little distraction can cause a catastrophe. God designed us to assist, aide and help. He gave us a detector to smell evil close up or far away. This special detector is called the Holy Spirit. We can not help anyone else if we are not being helped by the best.

Sometimes our family can not see the danger lurking ahead. Sometimes we as women can not see it but the Holy Spirit can. God will put on the emergency lights inside your spirit to let you know it's time to pray and react.

Women you can tell when your children meet the wrong friends. Something inside of you will light up like a firecracker. First you observe the situation until the emergency lights come on. Secondly, you will tell your child the company they are entertaining does not have their best interest at heart. Either they are haters (jealous), virginity thieves or spiritual rapist (using the word of God to manipulate a Christian back into a worldly life style). Whatever the situation your child is going through you begin to warn them before something happens. We hope our children listen the first time but if they don't we begin to pray. When praying pray the word of God. Speak victory scriptures over your circumstances. Let the devil know he is defeated. Most importantly believe what you say and pray. Women should take prayer seriously. Don't wait for the situation to end up in ICU before addressing it at the regular check up. When you have finished, identify the problem, pray in the Holy Spirit and believe what you pray will happen. God will loose the holy angels out of heaven on your behalf. The key to a praying woman is having a consistent prayer life. Never wait for the problem to come, stay prayed up before anything happens.

Beware of the prayer busters in your family's lives. They come to steal family, bible study and personal time with the Lord. Keep unity alive through prayer. My mom always taught me that seven days without prayer makes one weak. Keep your praying muscles built up.

How big are your spiritual muscles?

Spiritual Wheaties   Spiritual sugar puffs

Assisting your family through prayer is the best Christmas or birthday gift.

As a man and wife work together their unity generates a flow of the Holy Spirit to their children, home, job, relationships with others and most importantly with each other. Without unity of the man and woman there is no family. Some may disagree, but the broken pieces of families today have blown out of proportion. The spirit of divorce is devastating and consuming the body of Christ. Children are rebelling against their parents. For example, Little Johnny talks back and his parents want to reason with him. Did I mention that Johnny was seventeen years old? Little Johnny full of video games and volcano gossip slapped his mom. Little Johnny is diagnosed by a psychologist with ADD. (Attention Deficit Disorder) His parents, teachers and church do not want to put up with Little Johnny any longer because he's out of control. Little Johnny is kicked out of his parents home, put in a medical facility and then placed with a relative. I thought Jesus was a deliverer? Why do we wait to train our children until it's too late? This behavior Johnny is displaying could have been prevented when Johnny was three or four years old?

Let's meet another couple that enjoy reasoning with their children.

Meet Mr. & Mrs. Parker

Praise the Lord everybody! Our ten year old twins have been a blessing. Thanks to the bible we are able to access many helpful scriptures to help communicate with our children. We believe in communicating with our children according to the word of God. When our twins get out of order we quickly lay hands on them in the name of Jesus. Because the bible didn't specify where to lay our hands, we lay them on the legs, thighs and behind. We found this method of communication extremely effective. Once the twin's teachers told us the children were suffering with ADD. We were devastated. The teacher told us that the twins talked back, threw the chair and yelled "We don't care who you tell." Unfortunately, they were repeating another child's actions. As parents we came to the only conclusion, we had to cure the ADD with prayer, fasting and a swift kick in the right direction. There was some pleading, crying and pain but the twins were HEALED! The teacher was impressed the twins overcame the ADD so quickly. She asked us what method we used. We told her we took them to visit a well known psychologist by the name of Dr. Whoopabutt. The teacher wanted to know was the doctor facility local? We told her the doctor makes house visits which were convenient. The teacher inquired whether the doctor cured all types of ADD. We told her absolutely. We have access to the doctor 24 hours a day, seven days a week. Lastly, she asked us for the doctor's number. We told her it was 1-800-Whoopabutt Inc. Praise God for the bible the true Word of God!

The flow of the Holy Spirit is the key element needed to make the foundation of the family successful. Unfortunately, when the family stops becoming an example we are subject to liberalism, homosexuality, persons not believing in God, a rise in violence, sex, drugs and a host of ungodly things. We want our schools back and homosexuals to stop debating the right to be married. We the body of Christ must get back strong family values by adhering to the word of God. Here is a list of questions I want to ask:

1) When was the last time as husband and wife you prayed and read your bible together?
2) When is the last time you had bible study with your children?
3) When was the last time your family had dinner together?
4) Does your family pray before leaving the house?
5) Do you and your husband come in separate cars when you come to church?
6) As a married couple do you date each other and your children?
7) When is the last time you took a family vacation?
8) Whom and What do you spend most of your time with?
9) When was the last time your family told each other 'I love you'?
10) If you never saw your family again what is the one thing you would miss about them?
11) Do your children answer their elders by saying "yes sir, yes maam."

Today it seems more time is spent in church services than with our families. I intend at no time to put down the house of God. I believe the church building is a place for the body of Christ to come together to worship Jesus Christ and be revived. There must be a balance between the role of the church and the role of the family. Pastors, I'm pleading with you to maintain balance between family and church. When services in the church are exceeding time spent with family, it's time to cut back.

The family was established before the church. It's important to remember that your family is a blessing from God. Believer's, need to be taught to depend and lean on Jesus Christ for themselves. Believers must remember that their pastors are vessels being used by God to lead and direct them. Depending on your pastor and first ladies as savior is a violation of God's word. They are your shepherds not your gods. Pastors minister and teach the people of God to assist you in building God's kingdom, and emphasize you are not their Savior Christ the Lord. Through prayer and fasting God will bless you with an awesome team.

Some time ago, I was apart of a ministry whose leaders helped some of my family members backslide. The leaders encouraged some of my family members that a little leaven was alright. Before I knew it, the leader's I trusted to be in the word of God, were the ones destroying my family. It was like World War III! I was betrayed, hurt and blamed for my family members backsliding. I truly needed Jesus. I told the Lord, I served you, went to revivals, bible study, prayer, Sunday school, Sunday service, choir rehearsal, ushered, cleaned up the church and served on the kitchen committee. Why me? He said, why not you? What time did you spend with your family, and most of all me? I sat there dumbfounded. I was **WRONG!** I couldn't blame anyone but myself. If some of my family members were being overtaken it was because I was to busy to see it.

Never take your family for granted. I can't stress enough the importance of protecting your family by being unified. **(More unity more power!)**

The bible says in **Ephesians 4:26-27 'Be angry, and sin not: let not the sun go down upon your wrath: Neither give place to the devil.'**

Born Again families have given many places to the devil. They have allowed Satan to strip them of their birth right. Instead of addressing problems that affect their family, the problems are ignored and swept underneath the carpet. Bitterness, wrath, rejection, and wicked works begin to eat away the family's foundation and eventually cause cracks and water damage. Some foundations never recover.

Beware of cracks that can destroy the foundation. Never allow negative outside influence to become apart of your family. Snakes never make an announcement to bite, they attack without warning. In order to keep a solid, crack free foundation, its important to watch who you talk and walk with in the church. Men take your position and protect your wife and children. Stay fasted and prayed up. Wives intercede for your husband and children.

Saints keep your spiritual foundation solid and clear of cracks. Protect your family from the wolves. I've seen and heard so many horror stories about the believers destroying the believers. The foundation is severely damaged from a major flood of backbiting, lying and pride. Unfortunately when this demonic flood comes, it destroys every thing in its sight. Restoration, prayer and fasting, are some of the solutions of healing and rebuilding a severely damaged foundation.

Women, use your spiritual metal detector God has placed inside you to help assist your family. Children be obedient to your parents and lift them up in prayer. To believers who have no spiritual role models, pray and ask the Lord to send the right Godly persons in your life. These believers should be people who live a Godly lifestyle, help you reach your goals in Christ and watch out for your soul. God is always there waiting to hear from you. Cry out to Jesus and I guarantee he will help you!

THE CHURCH

Let's take a look at the church of today. Many people define the church as the building or the people but let's take a look at the different functions in the church free style. I would like to introduce the key players:

Church Alcoholic

Hi my name is Brother CA a.k.a Church Alcoholic. I know more about the church than I do my own family. I spend 99% of my time at the church. I love my job! The Pastor is always saying nice things about me. I clean-up the church, I work the parking lot, I open and close the church, I help the food committee serve food, I'm on the usher board, deacon board and the youth assistant. I know there's more people lined up for my positions but I feel I do a better job because I've been here so long. I have to take so much medicine for high blood pressure, diabetes, eczema, heart disease and arthritis. I know God is a healer. I'm working in the church and he see's what I do and that's what makes me blessed. I told my family we have to make sacrifices for the Lord. I hope to see you soon! You come and visit me in the rest home, I mean the church house. Praise the Lord and pray my healing, I mean strength in the Lord!

Deacon Function

Hi! I mean Praise the Lord! My name is Deacon Function. I am in charge of keeping you at church all day. I make sure you don't spend time with your families. It's great fun when the Pastor and Wife don't have time for each other. The church goes down, chaos arises and much more. It is truly a joy to see the saints come in for the choir concerts. The entertainment, I mean ministry is awesome. I don't know the last time I've seen people so competitive, I mean flowing in the Holy Spirit. We had a great time last month. We had Sunday school @ 9am, Sunday Service at 11:00 a.m., and church let out at 3p.m. We came back at 4:30 p.m. for the usher board service and came back for 7 p.m. evening service. Next week will be the same services but I forgot we have a choir concert to. See yaw there.

Bro. & Sister Counsel

Hi! I mean Praise Him! We are Bro. & Sister Counsel. We are counseling leaders at our church. We enjoy hearing the problems of our hurt brothers and sisters. We pray for them and occasionally fast one meal. We take the time before prayer to call our friends in the gospel to help us pray for the hurt, distorted and broken hearted saints. We call the people like the idol gossiping mother board, First Lady tell it all, Bro. Nosy, Sister spread it and lastly Sister never forgive. We make sure your information stays confidential with them and ourselves. There is someone that's here for you at all times. Please call us anytime. We are here to help. Remember our number is **1-800-We tell it all.**

Youth Director live it like you feel it!

Hey! I said What's up! I am here for the youth. I make sure their parents don't know what they tell me. So what they have sex. The parents did it in their days. I'm still trying to get over temptation but hey God loves me anyway. I'm over the youth because I can relate to them. I really love to help the youth hide their feelings Alleluia!! Youth are here for a second so why not help them cut off their life line so they can live their life like they want. What is obedience? It's doing what you want to do. I hate when preachers twist the word of God. Hey youth I'm waiting for you! Be yourself!

Elder Show Off

Praise Him! You know you were looking at my fine suit when I walked in late to Sunday service. Stop pretending you're not jealous of me. I have confidence, charisma, and a sense of humor. I can't help it if I'm the one and only Elder that has it like this. People look up to me as their example. I am the answer to their problems. The Lord called me to the women especially. He called me to the men to, but the women he really called me to. I understand their pain, hurt and sensitive side. That's my gift. I am the Elder. Hey what's your problem? Tell me all about it and I will be there in a flash. Men must make an appointment first. Women I do only house calls for you. You're just too delicate to come out at night that just wouldn't be right. You like that rhyme . . . I'll do that for you anytime. I am . . . the Elder.

Super Spiritual

Praise da Lord! I see visions, I dream dreams. I prophelie . . . I mean prophesy. The one good thing about me is that I always slip in the truth here and there. I remember over hearing this couples conversation while at a prayer meeting. The husband asked the wife were they separated. The word of the Lord came to me in a vision that the couple wanted to divorce. I found out the next day that the couple was talking about their laundry. I misinterpreted that just a little but I knew I was close. The husband wanted to make sure the whites were with the whites and the colored with the coloreds. The Lord showed me right there the couple was prejudice. I found out later they were still talking about their laundry. I don't care what people say I was still right! Alleluia! I tell you God has anointed me for this last hour to tell people the truth. The truth or a lie will set you free. I see another vision coming . . . Uh Oh here it comes . . . !!!!

Music Ministry

I am the most popular leader in the church. I can change the mood of the church any time I get ready. Everyone depends on me. People come from all over the world just to hear the jamming music. Do you know I am more popular in the church than the preacher? Even Sister Off Beat can't run around the church without the beat. You know Da . . . Na . . . Na . . . Na. It's amazing to see people doing their own thing in the church. I can make them feel good, bad and super sad. I have so much in common with Lucifer (Satan). He plays people all the time and we in the music ministry do to. Come join the choir and I guarantee the force will be with you.

Bishop and First Lady

Praise God, Praise God. We are the Bishop and First Lady. Our leaders and congregation appreciate us. Although this may be Bishops 3rd marriage and

First lady second marriage doesn't mean anything. I know God said a Bishop must be blameless, a husband of one wife at a time. (I Timothy 3:2) Honey snorkel, I'm so glad you brought that up. So even though I'm your third wife does that still make me the First Lady. Baby cakes you will always be my First Lady. Oh snicker bear you are my love care bear. Now you all come down to our church where we believe in twisting the word of God just a little but not a whole lot.

When a Pastor & his wife are called to pastor a flock, God impregnates them with vision. The ministry is birthed through the people God sends to the ministry. As shepherds of a flock it's extremely important to create balance. Church members must be taught the depths of their loyalty to God, their family and then the church.

In order to have a healthy church, the members must have productive lives with their families. The way they act with their family will determine how they treat the church. It's so easy for families to neglect the cares of each other through position at the church. Often times the result of people not getting the proper attention from their families causes them to seek attention or praise through their position in the church. Pastors' and first ladies I want to encourage you to teach the people of God he's blessed you with to be on guard of the enemy's devices. Position when given is to build God's kingdom not to elevate oneself. Once a person attaches themselves to the church position they begin to elevate the position higher than God and unfortunately the position is no longer a ministering tool but an idol.

Don't abuse your position. God uses your gifts and abilities to reach those who do not know him. Exercise your gifts and talents by allowing God to direct your steps. God is waiting for someone with an attitude of humility, concern for his people, a love for his word and an attitude of praise and worship. Without God we are nothing. He made us something when he went to the cross for us. I heard a preacher say we have the most expensive gift in the cheapest container. What a great illustration. I thank God for taking our inabilities and using them for his glory.

As saints of God we must remember to maintain our spiritual position in Christ. Spend quality time with Jesus. Before your day begins, start by telling God how much you love and adore him. Make a list of attributes to describe Jesus. Call them out in your daily prayer. Worship is telling Jesus who he is to you. Praise is telling Jesus what he's done for you. Once you have established relationship with Christ you can then establish relationship with your family and the church.

God has left the most precious thoughts with us in his word. He tells us how to live, walk, talk and guide our lives. The Word of God is the essential tool we need to be successful. Stop depending on the church to be your security blanket, money, hope and main resource. Stop blaming Sister Peppermint Patty for your life being in shambles when you can call on Jesus and he will send the right help to deliver you out of the situation. Stop depending on anyone or thing and start leaning on the Master Jesus Christ our Lord and Savior.

The role of the church was never set up for perfection but helps work the imperfection out of us through the word of God. God called leaders who have the guiding hand of the Holy Spirit to help resurrect us from death into light. When the lady touched Jesus garment it was her faith in him that made her whole. How much faith do we really have? Do we have more faith in man than in Christ? God forbid. If you have been leaning and depending on the church to be your savior repent. If you have been waiting for Sister Macaroni and Cheese to smile at you every Sunday and all you get is a frown, repent. We as saints of God should have the power to break through demonic forces that hinder God's church from growing.

There was an older sister in the church that would come in and play the tambourine like crazy. She would beat it so hard it looked as if her hand would fall off any day. My friends and I would laugh at her and talk about the way she played. We assumed she was playing like that to get attention and be seen by everyone. One day I asked her sarcastically, why do you play the tambourine like you're on fire? These were the words she spoke, "The Lord has brought me from a mighty long way. I lost my home, my children and lost all hope. God told me he would never leave me nor forsake me. My days were so darkened I couldn't see light and I wasn't blind. But God touched me and I had never experienced a peace like that in my life. It's a peace that's indescribable. It's so true when the song says a peace that surpasses all of your understanding. I got my joy back, I got a new song and the Lord blessed me with a church family that supported me. I even thank the enemies that talked about me because I knew they didn't understand but I would never wish the tragedy I went through on anyone. That's why I play my tambourine so hard and sincerely. God bless you child. Thank you for not assuming because assuming is a lie. Thank you for coming to me and asking me for yourself."

Wow! That blew my entire mind out of the window. I became apart of the famous category called hypocrite. (Talking about my brother or sister in a negative way) Don't ever assume, get the facts from the individual. The Holy Spirit will let you know if they're not telling the truth. This sister was telling the truth. My life was positively changed. What a great testimony!

The church is the body of Christ. Are you walking in your call? Are you waiting for that special attention? Are you spreading disease through out the body of Christ through neglecting your family, idol gossiping, lack of time spent with the Lord, bad attitude, procrastination etc . . . etc . . . ? Can you imagine one of your diseases could cause someone to miss the opportunity to accept Jesus Christ as Lord and Savior? Is that you? God help us!

Say this prayer if you have hindered the body of Christ through selfish motives:

Dear Lord Jesus,

I confess my sins before you and ask you to forgive me for the things I have said, done and thought wrong against the body of Christ. Lord Jesus I have not been the example you have called me to be and I have been hindering the body of Christ by_____. Please help me to be a better person and love my brothers and sisters with a sincere heart. I am your willing and humbled servant. I rebuke satan and his demonic powers trying to influence me to do wrong and tear down God's kingdom. I want to build God's kingdom through a fasted, prayed and Christ like life style. Thank you Lord Jesus, for redeeming, strengthening and helping me to seek you first. In Jesus mighty and majestic name I pray. Amen!

LARGE MINISTRIES VS. SMALL MINISTRIES

In most large ministries the pastors/bishops are usually untouchable, never having the time to greet their members because it's too many of them. Unfortunately, the individuals that receive the pastors/bishops attention are those who started in the early stages of the ministry with the pastor/bishop. Most leaders of the ministry keep you from getting close to the Man of God fearing other believers want their position. I want to emphasize that this happens in most large ministries. Secondly, it's shameful to say that many believers don't want to pay the price for the time sacrificed to develop the ministry. It's sad to say they want the glory but not the pain. Another key issue in most large ministries is hidden sin. Holding a position with hidden sin is easy because it's so many people to hide with. A believer in a large ministry can have a luke warm mentality but it takes a longer time to be detected.

Most small Ministries are relationship based. They know everybody and everybody knows them. Most small ministries deal with the rift raft of discord, jealousy, strife, contention and everything else but on a larger scale. When observing smaller ministries you see the skeletons immediately. It will not take long for Sister Idol Gossip to find out what it is your doing. Most leaders will throw stones at everyone except themselves. It's a crying shame. It's awful to say that if you are not following man's law you can and will be excommunicated quickly. Mind Control is strongly enforced and backed up by scriptures. The love is shown in the beginning but once you get to know other believers it gets very cold.

The difference between large and small ministries is one ministry is large and the other small. The both go through problems and experience the same level of difficulty. It's funny to say that even the building funds, tithes and offerings experiences are close to the same caliber. When a building fund is called the people disappear until all the work is completed. Most saints are lazy and want to pick and choose what to give in reference to money. Tithes and offerings are a joke!!! Believers want to use any excuse not to give to God. The money is to further the kingdom of God and take care of the man of God. Instead believers want to dictate how God's money is used. They'll want their tithes to be used on the gas bill but expect the church lights to come on by faith. If we had to depend on most believers faith to turn on the lights we would definitely be in the dark! Most people dislike pastors who call the **'unbelief offering lines'** or better known as the **'auctions lines.'** Let me explain.

"Praise the Lord Saints."

"Praise the Lord Pastor."

"Well it's offering time."

"Boooooo!"

"Alright, I hope I didn't hear no negative talking."

"No Pastor."

"Amen Saints."

"Let me have the people who have $20.00 stand in the right aisle. The $50.00 folks stand in the left aisle. Lastly, the people with $100.00 or more stand in the middle aisle."

"What if you only have $1.00-5.00 pastor?"

"Now you know you spend more on eBay. You ought to be ashamed of yourself asking that question. I need some serious folks. Now can I get $250.00, what about $225 . . . $200? I see a hand."

Yolanda Gilliam

"I have it Pastor!!!"

"Sold to Sister Jenkins. Oh the Lord got a special blessing for you. Today you get a special prayer and blessing from me."

"Oh pastor thank you!!!!"

"I wish I had won the offering auction. I really didn't have it. I really could have used a blessing. I have so many bills, my children are acting up and I know God only blesses those based on how much money they have. Lord, please help me be rich so I can be blessed!"

What a shame that people are no longer looked upon as saved born again believers but how much they save in the bank. Tithes and Offerings are essential to a believers walk. A believer never wants to miss the opportunity to be a blessing to the house of the Lord. We do not want God's people misinterpreting how to give their tithes and offering to the ministry of God. As believers, exploiting God's people and creating discord is something God hates and will not tolerate. We as believers say God said this and that but truthfully speaking it's us that's doing all the talking not God. In our ministries we need to give the altar call like we do the offering auctions. I'm sure souls would come in if we take that as serious as offering time. Lord help us to make your house a house of prayer and not a den of auctions and thievery.

Ministries are no longer ministries but businesses. Has the body of Christ gotten so busy to notice the needs of one another? Why do we count our members as mutual investments instead of people of God who need their souls to be fed? Why do believers expect the church to be their Jesus? Check out these comments believers make when they want their way.

- The pastor forgot to mention how well I cooked for the appreciation service so I'm leaving the church.
- I called the church to let them know I was sick in the hospital but no one came to visit so I'm not speaking to the pastor for thirty days.
- I couldn't attend bible study because I hit my toe on the bedroom door but no one from the church called to check on me.
- The pastor's wife sure looks good. I wish my wife looked like that.

36

- I wish my husband would treat me good like pastor. I'm sick of being treated like a dog.
- They look at me so mean they probably don't like me.
- Don't hate because you don't drive a car like mine. You probably are in sin that's why you don't have what I have or more.

Don't ever think that our Pastors/Leaders don't have something to say about the members.

- My Goodness, baby sure got some back.
- Why is that nasty woman sitting in the first row half naked?
- Usher board make sure your best friend sits where you want them and everybody else has to sit where you tell them.
- Don't smile at them they will think you want their husband or wife.
- They are not going to take my position. I worked to hard for it. I had to pretend I liked people just to get it.
- I know they do not think they are going to join the choir looking and smelling like that!

I'm sure you can think of more things to say but this is enough! Believers have the nerve to talk about slavery. We are enslaving each other with our ridiculous behavior.

Matthew 21: 12-13

And Jesus went into the temple of God, and cast out all them that sold and bought in the temple, and overthrew the tables of the moneychangers, and the seats of them that sold doves, and said unto them, It is written, My house shall be called the house of prayer but ye have made it a den of thieves.

In Matthew 21:12-13 Jesus addressed the issues pertaining to selling things in the house of God. The church has become one great commercial. More sells but lesser miracles. People definitely want to prosper but they don't want to live righteous lives.

As believers our attention should be directed to those who need the Lord. Jesus said in **Mark 16:15 'Go ye into all the world, and preach the**

gospel to every creature.' Maybe we have been interpreting the scripture incorrectly. Did it say, 'Go ye into all the churches, telling each other off, be a busy body, divorce your Godly husband or wife in the church, compromise etc . . . . oh yeah!!! Don't forget to tell this to every creature.'

Sometimes what believers say and do is contrary to God's word. It's time to read and apply God's word to our daily lives. Jesus focus was to those who were lost not to those who were saved. What is the body of Christ looking at? What are we as believers looking for? Are we looking at what the other is doing or souls needing salvation?

In conclusion whether a ministry is large or small believers need to be sensitive to the needs of their brothers and sisters.

People before business and self!

FUNCTIONS IN THE CHURCH

Functions in church should always be balanced. Many functions in the church are smoke screens. The church (building) is a place for believers in Christ to come together to worship and praise the Lord. In doing this we become stronger and closer to our brothers and sisters. Because the devil is out to kill, steal and destroy his main purpose is to keep your mind off of the things of God.

Most believers believe that coming to church saves them despite how they walk with Christ. In observing today's ministries the church is now a vehicle being used to introduce the latest style of clothing, music, foods, hang outs etc. The devil no longer has to distract the body of Christ with the world's agenda we as believers do enough to ourselves. Because believers in CHRIST have allowed, permitted, accepted and glorified the world in the church, we have become heroes to our enemies and unbelievers.

Non-believers don't feel threatened by the church because we have let down our standard of righteous living and opened the door to compromise. The devil has taken the body of Christ to the mountain (Matthew 4:8-9), showed us beautiful things and we have embraced this angel of light with open arms. GOD HELP US!

Believers in Christ, begin to spend time with the Lord and your families. Pastors teach families how to remain a family first. Stop encouraging divorce, leaving the church, excommunication, respect of persons and enforce strength and love. Without Jesus we can do nothing. Stop burning your pastor out with 15 appreciation services per month, 500 choir concerts and usher board programs. Stop allowing the families in your ministry to disrespect each other by making functions in the church more important than family time. Members, ministry workers and leaders stop burdening the pastor with excuses not to support the ministry. If the pastor needs your assistance at bible study or prayer meeting be there. Believers in Christ, stop showing up to all the choir musicals and BBQ's. Grow up in Jesus name!

We have a responsibility to Jesus Christ and our pastors. Most pastors listen to the leading of the Holy Spirit. Saints stop having a rebellious spirit. Stop trying to control the ministry because your tithes and offerings are generous. We are a team fighting against the same enemy but the enemy should not be each other.

Function after Junction can burn your ministry down to the ground. Most families don't know each other anymore. They spend more time at evening service than at home. They spend more time at Friday night service than reading the Word of God. Most saints that spend that much time going to church have no vision, no life and no focus.

I petition the body of Christ to ask themselves, what do you value most about your family? What drives you to do the things you do for them? Do you treat your family and church family like Jesus? How much quality time do you spend with your Lord? When is the last time you told your Pastor you appreciate him? When is the last time you sent your Pastor and First Lady on a paid vacation? How often do you bless the man and woman of God?

When we bless the man and woman of God we are furthering God's kingdom. People need to know they are appreciated not popular. Any one can be popular but what about appreciated. Take the time and really ask yourself, 'Am I being a light for Jesus?' Some of our co-workers are afraid to get saved because they think their life will be taken from their families and dedicated to the usher board 24 hours. We make church look pretty scary sometimes. Some women have left their husbands to be dedicated to their Pastor. We as the body of Christ need to check ourselves. We need to prioritize quickly. Jesus is coming for a church not individuals or a select group of holy rollers. He is coming for his bride. He is not coming for Sister Division, Bro. discord or Evangelist Tell Me About It. He is coming for a bride who is on one accord, one mind and one spirit. Is that you?

PK ACADEMY AWARDS

Welcome to the PK Academy Awards. Ladies and gentleman you are in for a great treat tonight. As you know tonight's awards will honor some of the greatest PK stars known in the church world today. Introducing your host for this grand occasion is:

Evangelist SomeTimey

"Thank you, Thank you. Good evening Ladies and gentleman. It gives me great pleasure to introduce the winners for this evenings PK awards."

Deacon Sour Puss

Hey, I mean Praises to God and all that. I am Deacon Sour Puss. I'm on the Usher Board. I hate it when people try to sit where they want to sit. I am quick to say "Get your tired, disobedient self back over here and sit down right here". I don't play. I am one mean machine. If a woman's skirt is short, I will give the most evil look at that nasty thang, it's meaner than the devil and he's one ugly thing. I will take a quick look at them pretty legs. I ain't blind and I still got some livin in me. Anyway praise the Lord. I am glad to get a PK award tonight. It's about time my Pastor recognized me. Through my hospitable ways I caused many to leave the church but I had to protect my church pews. Thank ya!

Evangelist Roller Eyes

Heylleluia! That's me Evangelist Roller Eyes. I would like to thank the First Lady for encouraging me to be myself. If it wasn't for her I don't know where

I would be. I can't stand for people to look at me like they are something and I'm not. I have been saved for 10 years and I still have a ways to go. I ain't perfect but I ain't tryin to be. If you want me to speak I have to know you first. This lady came up to me and was so friendly. She said hello and I rolled my eyes and told her I don't know you and don't try to come up in here and talk to me. This new member had the nerve to sit in my seat at church!!! I rolled my eyes, pointed to Deacon Sour Puss and he handled that with quickness! My eyes got stuck one day because my husband asked me to make him a sandwich like I was his slave. I told him I'm your wife not your slave. People are crazy that's why I keep them backed off by rolling my eyes. First lady, thank you for nominating me for this award. I know you're not trying to rush me off the mic. That's why I roll my eyes now!!!!!!

Sister Didn't, Can't and Won't Speak

Whatever!!! Don't hate because it's hard for you to ignore when you ain't part of the church group. Sister Know she can sing better than me tried to be friendly once again. I gave her the look. You know the look. I said to myself she got one more time to be friendly and I'm going show her what the word friendly means. I can't believe Trisha was trying to join the choir and take my place. That ain't even happening. She better back off. She got to earn her stripes just like I earned mine. I am not talking to her for 5 more years than maybe we will let her in the group. Do you know that Balina had the nerve to wear a cute outfit? Everyone was saying how cute she was I was so mad because they didn't say nothing about mines. I did not look her way for 6 months. She asked me what was wrong I gave her the hand. Back off Balina!!!!! You got to take charge. Don't let anyone run over you. I'm glad I got something for being rude. It's about time. My nick name is moody booty!!!! That's alright. Don't hate, appreciate.

Evangelist Hoop and Holler

What's up in the church!!!! I can holler and hoop. The ladies are so generous to nominate me for this grand occasion. I am thrilled. Every time the music plays there I am. This man had the nerve to get saved. He was crying loud before the Lord!! I was so mad. I started speaking in tongues and prophesying louder than a train whistle. I won that match. I don't play! I don't care if someone is getting saved don't ever be louder than me. People started taking their eyes off me and putting their attention on him and Jesus. What's worse he was sincere and I wasn't. That really burned me up. Obviously, I'm doing a great job. I'm at the awards aren't I?

Brother Hog the Mic

I am a hog for mic's. I love to eat them up. Sister Jan tried to lead a song. It was her turn to lead but I didn't feel it. You know that thing called the anointing. I grabbed her mic and started singing my heart out. I was out of tune but that's because I didn't know all the words. She had no spirit I had all of them. I'll never forget that. It bothers me when people try to be sincere about what it is they're singing. One time the Pastor was preaching but he wasn't breaking it down like he should have. I grabbed that mic and started preaching and prophesying. Do you know they were so jealous of me that they made me go to another church? Isn't that something? I thank you new age church for nominating me to get this PK award. Hey give me the mic back I have something to say. It will only take about 2 more hours.

Mr. & Mrs. Fight it Out

Hey Everybody I can't believe you picked humble old us. I love my wife. She shows she loves me every day. The usher came and gave me my little handkerchief because it fell out my pocket. My wife turned around and busted her right in her face. She had only been at the church for three months but she had to show her you don't mess with my bar of pudding. Oh honey, I was only doing what the bible says. You protect me too. Remember when we went to the fellowship hall and the cook gave me a small wing. Yes sweet heart I do. You gave him a black eye for it right in church. That was such a blessing. We are such great examples. Honey I'll never forget arguing with them other Christians at the car wash because they offered us a track about Jesus. They said they couldn't tell we were saved because we were beating up the attendant at the car wash for not giving us a discount. Thank you for this gracious award. Keep living humble like us!

Prophetic Minister Hidden Jealousy

I can see you! I know that in your heart you are like me. You wish you had everything another person had. You smile but if people really saw your smile it would spell E-V-I-L. I have heard that people don't like me because I pretend I'm happy for them but in essence I'm NOT! I wish it was me with the new car and new clothes. Sometimes, I wish some people would die so I can get some of the spot light. I crave recognition. I hate it when people don't recognize me even though I didn't do anything to deserve it. Can you believe someone is trying to be me? I can!

Pastor and Sister Picky

Praise the Lord Mighty Saints! We're not talking to you; we're talking to the football team. Now we are talking to you! Praise the Lord Saints of God! I hate it when you do not respond. God is? Tell them honey! Say, God is good! Honey they don't know what you're thinking. They should! I don't like people telling me nothing. I am the king of this castle. People tell me they have a calling, I am their calling. What do you know about Jesus? He talks to me not to you. I will let you know when he is speaking to you. Stop whining about needing prayer. I am watching the game, I pray for you at church. You saints act like this is my only profession. I have a life to. I love Golfing, movies, eating out, taking vacations, skiing and then preaching. Preaching is last because it takes all my energy. I am doing God a favor. Give me a break! Hec, he died for you. I'm here to watch and spend God's money. Getting tithes and offerings keeps me motivated to stay in the church house. Isn't that right honey? That's right Cuddle bear!!! Thanks for the award. Do we get paid for coming to this mess? I don't do anything for free!

Youth Minister Dr. DR

Dr. DR stands for dreadful and ridiculous. The youth are the youth of today!!!! Why do people lie and say that? The youth are going to get old and have crackly bones. Anyways, I want the youth to do something for me. To keep the devil from getting into your mind of intelligence do this little exercise. 1-2-3—put the IPOD in the ears!!!! That's right!!! If you want to keep the devil from coming in put the IPOD in the ears!!! It's also a way to drown out your parent's lousy annoying voice, your teacher giving a homework assignment and the pastor preaching. You can put 500 to 1000 songs in the IPOD but only hear one song at a time. The majority of IPOD users only listens to an average of one hundred songs and downloads over 1000. It doesn't make sense but it sure is cool. Born Again youth are rarely taught the importance of being goal oriented, becoming a homeowner or a visionary. Most youth mentors/leaders tell the youth to pursue their dreams by looking at them. Most mentors/leaders still rent homes, talk faith but don't apply it and instill negative principles of defeat in the youth of today by their example. The majority of youth are not pursuing a college education or an entrepreneurship career. The most hilarious part of born again youth is they pursue their master's degree in watching TV., Ph. D. talking on the hellphone . . . I mean cell phone and a bachelor's degree spending money on clothes. Unfortunately, this generational curse will follow their children. Isn't that wonderfully dreadful?"

PK's are the number one killers of the church today!!! Pastors Kids? NO!!! **Position Killers**! The church members are so dedicated in making sure no one takes their place in their ministry. I guess that's what's wrong it's their ministry and not God's. Christians are no longer trying to talk to people about getting saved but about leaving the church. When believers feel threatened their position is going to be filled by a more qualified person they begin to act out and start the PK war!!! When is the body of Christ going to grow up? Jesus wants to come back for a church without spot or wrinkles. How many spots and wrinkles do you have? Iron them out through the word of God.

When God has called you, he called you as one who is unique and special. The body of Christ is a team who enhances each other. No one can out do the other if we are one. God gave you special qualities to build his church not tear it down. If you are suffering with PK disease than admit it, fast and pray the desire to transform into a more Godly character. Don't let Satan deceive you that your calling is not important. Jealousy kills and destroys at the roots. It's a deadly disease.

People will kill, manipulate and destroy because of it. It is a dear cousin to the PK (position killer). When your position makes you feel that you're above others then pride makes it's home in your life. Satan had the same problem. He wanted to be like God but then he wanted to be God. Of course his end is destruction. PK's end will also end in terrible destruction. Stop manipulating the usher board. Don't manipulate your position by letting your favorite people sit where they want and the ones you don't like sit where you want. Respect of persons is not a Godly characteristic but that of evil. Preachers stop preaching people over the pulpit. Go to the person and let them know you have an ought with them. Don't use your authority in an evil manner. God will punish you. Its better that you learn to discipline yourself before God does.

RESTORATION OF THE BODY OF CHRIST

The body of Christ is in desperate need of restoration. It appears as though everything is alright but it's not. Unfortunately, Jesus was all we needed and depended on. Today we feel as though Jesus needs us more than we need him. Unfortunately, we as believers have sought the advice of secular counseling services, talk shows, coffee and medicine just to cope with every day life.

The bible is a wonderful book written to help believers live a productive, spiritual and physical life. In **II Timothy 3:16-17** it says:

> **All scripture is given by inspiration of God, and is profitable for doctrine, for reproof, for correction, for instruction in righteousness:**

> **That the man of God may be perfect, thoroughly furnished unto all good works.**

God said every single scripture in the bible is to help better our Christian walk with him. Let's take a look at the meaning of II Timothy 3:16-17 and **BREAK IT DOWN!!!!**

Every highly, accurate, sacred writing of the bible is a supernatural divine influence of sacred writers, prophets and apostles. These individuals were qualified to communicate moral and religious truth with authority by God. The bible is a benefit of teachings that make known it's disapprovals but helps a believer add or subtract to make things right. The word of God teaches and directs the man/woman of God to have all parts of his spiritual and physical being in harmony with a common purpose. In addition the man/woman of God should live a life of holiness, purity, equity, justice, integrity, honesty and faithfulness. Lastly, a Christian's walk should display God's word through every action, word spoken and thought with the interest of conforming to a standard of right behavior.

As a believer every answer you need is in the bible. We don't need inspirational talk shows, secular talk shows or a quick coffee fix. All we need is Jesus. God gave us Godly instructors to teach us the ways of God. First he gave us the Holy Spirit who directs us to the right individuals who will impart God's work in us to be restored.

Restoration is not always instant. Some situations take more time. Please don't compare your situation with someone else. The old statement is never be quick to cast a stone because that same stone may pop you in your head. Some believers have never experienced one of their children going to jail or a husband or wife leaving them. Most of these believers are quick to put on their Judge Judy clothes and show no mercy. When the trouble making demons come visiting these same believers they want to put on sack cloth, ashes, justify the situation, blame the devil and other believers who they think are going against them. How quickly we forget what we say. Like my mom says today you can dish it but you can't take it when the shoe is on the other foot. Restoration is the process of bringing an object back to its original state. Isn't it time we help bring each other back to life? Like the song says Speak life not death.

When seeking the Lord for a husband or wife you have to be sure your past hurts and disappointments have been properly healed. Some people are still carrying negative baggages. Some of the baggage's saints still carry are:

1) I can't let some of my past relationships go.
2) Unforgiveness
3) Married and divorced many times in the church
4) I'm saved but I just don't have the faith anymore
5) My fire for God died out a long time ago
6) Discouragement
7) I still like my best friend's husband or wife in a lover's way. I'm saved but I'm still struggling in that area.

8) I think it's greener over there across the fence. **(Try watering your own lawn!!)**
9) I'm always late, people understand that's the way I am.
10) I feel so defeated.
11) I'm afraid maybe I should stop watching Fear Factor!!!
12) Lazy for Jesus. I have to work, shop and look at the stories on TV. I don't have time to read one scripture or tell someone about Jesus. Oh here comes my man to take me out. This is another reason why I can't go to bible study.
13) Complaining

Very few believers of God carry the Restoration suitcase. Restoration is an essential key to helping your fallen brothers or sisters come back to Jesus. Christian believers can help each other with a testimony, encouraging word and a listening ear. You can't be restored if you don't read your bible. I call the Saints who read their bibles occasionally full time spiritual sleepers.

Have you tried to communicate with someone who spoke a different language? It's hard. Sometimes you try to find a word or object that both of you are familiar with but the communication barrier is extremely difficult to understand. In order for you to understand the other person's language you have to study and master it. We as believers have to master and study the word of God. We want to recognize when God is speaking to us or when he wants to bless us. We will miss many blessings because we do not know or follow the word of God. He is looking for those who look like him through their walk and talk. Can he find you?

Are you hiding from God through lies, a form of godliness, a cursing mouth, negative attitude, home wrecker, disobedient child, evil eye, first lady gossiper, back biting preacher, treating people indifferently, unloving usher, critical choir or the abusive husband and wife?

God help restore the body of Christ to love you and help us to love each other.

Have you taken your eyes off of Jesus? How long does it take before you begin to doubt your master? Why do you limit what he can do for you? Are you asking for something that doesn't belong in your destiny?

God is watching out for you. Begin to get quiet and I guarantee he will hear your voice. Sincerity, Commitment and Faith will drive Jesus to listen to your prayers. God wants you and your situations to be restored.

Some Christian's situations have been in the grave for years. Isn't it time those situations were resurrected from death to life. Stop being afraid and embrace change for the better. Your family, self and unsaved loved ones need restoring. Be restored in the name of Jesus!

The body of Christ has weakened their position with the spirit of compromise. It would be nice for every saint to prosper financially. Unfortunately, some Christians need to have better attitudes in order to keep the money God wants to bless them with. I can understand why God says in his word to let your mind be renewed by his word.

The body of Christ needs to be restored back to holiness, a respect for God's house, his leadership, and most of all saints need to put the family back in first position.

THE TEMPLE

The temple, church or house of God as we call it today is a place where believers in Christ come together to worship our Lord and Savior Jesus Christ. It is a place of peace and safety.

Most religions around the world especially those out side of the Christian born again church take their places of worship very seriously. When you enter the temples or synagogues there is an extreme reverence and respect for God. In these religious synagogues the people pray continuously, women and men are covered by veils or robes exposing none of their body. In addition to the high reverence of respect for their temple they are in one accord and one mind.

The prayer prayed in the synagogues last for hours and sometimes days. Children are trained from an early age to learn the laws of religion, prayer but most importantly God is put first in everything. Some of these people religious beliefs are so serious that they are willing to kill and die for what they believe in. The synagogue symbolizes holiness, sacred worship and admonishing their God. There are no other activities allowed in the temple but prayer, praise and worship to their God.

Born Again believers places of worship have a more diverse way of doing things in the house of God. In the born again believers churches we find that there is more leisure in dress wear, types of music played and performances. The old church is constantly ridiculed for putting more biblical emphasis on the outer appearance of man and less biblical emphasis on the inner man. The new church is praised for putting more emphasis on the inner man than the outer man.

Whether outward or inner appearance both areas of a believer's life are important and must be addressed according to God's word. When you build a relationship with Jesus the inner man begins to change and form a lifestyle of holiness. As these changes occur, the outside and inside appearance reflects the Holy Spirit of a believer's life.

The bible says in **I John 2:15 'Love not the World, neither the things that are in the world. If any man love the world, the love of the Father is not in him.'** As a believer in Christ it is our Godly responsibility to take on the characteristics of Christ. We should no longer look or act like the world but our walk should exemplify a Godly way of life.

Believers are prohibited from taking away or adding to the word of God. Music and clothing is one of the biggest controversies in the church today. Should the body of Christ allow secular dancing, beat boxing, hip hop, rap, praise dancing and stomping in the church? Should born again women wear pants, tank tops, mini skirts etc. in the church. Truthfully speaking the type of music played and clothing worn in most churches today has gotten out of control. Let's take a look from a biblical stand point.

Because we are God's peculiar people it is important that we maintain a different lifestyle than the world.

In I Peter 2:9-11, **'But ye are a chosen generation, a royal priesthood, an holy nation, a peculiar people; That ye should show forth the praises of him who have called you out of darkness into his marvelous light: Which in time past were not a people, but are now the people of God: Which had not obtained mercy, but now have obtained mercy. Dearly beloved, I beseech you as strangers and pilgrims, abstain from fleshly lusts, which war against the soul; KJV**

Let's take a look at this same verse **I Peter 2:9-11** in the Amplified Version.

'But you are a chosen race, a royal priesthood, a dedicated nation, {God's} own purchase, special people, that you may set forth the wonderful deeds and display the virtues and perfections of him who called you out of darkness into his marvelous light. Once you were not a people {at all} but you are now God's people; once you were unpitied, but now you are pitied and have receive mercy.

Beloved, I implore you as aliens and strangers and exiles {in this world} to abstain from the sensual urges (the evil desires, the passion of the flesh, your lower nature) that wage war against the soul.'

Peculiar means strange, unusual or specific. It also means that people can tell that it's something different about you. As a believer our life should be different from the world's way of talking, walking, music and dress wear. It even means that we should not eat some of the same foods as the world. In the book of Daniel the three Hebrew boys did not eat from the same table as the King and his servants. The bible says that their countenances appeared fairer, fatter and flushed than all the children which ate at the Kings table. The King depended on Daniel and three Hebrew boys for wisdom and understanding instead of his wise men and astrologers.

We as believers have no business leaning on the world for advice, enjoying their music and dressing our royal priestly bodies in the world's clothing. Most churches have allowed the world's beat in their places of worship. Non-believers no longer have a fear of respect for God's house but feel comfortable coming and staying as they are. The church has conformed to the ways of ungodly living but calling it God's way of doing things in the new generation.

Music has hypnotized the churches of today with a wave of deception and misleading of God's holiness. God said come out from among them and be ye separate says the Lord. The church says, "Blend in; God understands we are the new church doing things with a new flavor and charisma."

There is no conviction. There are swords and chains drawn when you do not go along with the new trend better known as the New Age Movement. This new movement has leaked and sneaked the world's way of doing things in our churches. We no longer stand against unrighteousness but we welcome it with open arms. Please understand me I am speaking to the church, born again believers who know who Jesus is. The seasoned saints of God have a responsibility to represent the kingdom of God with respect and honor.

Women's dress wear is out of control in the church. Once I was told my skirt was to long but it was 3 inches below my knees. I was encouraged by a leader to wear my skirt short because I was young. What happened to the elders teaching the younger men and women how to live and represent a righteous life in Christ? Showing cleavage is the delicacy in the house of God. No longer is our attention on prayer, praise and worship but on legs, thighs and breasts. The appetite of the world has become a spiritual cancer of the church and unfortunately its slowly eating the body of Christ. There are so many excuses for performing in the church. Another excuse used by the church allowing these types of performances is that these performances draw in the youth.

The bible says in **Proverbs 22:6 'Train up a child in the way he should go: and when he is old, he shall not depart from it.'**

Young people would not know a lot of what was going on if their parents and seasoned saints did not allow it or teach them. We use the young people as an excuse so we can get our soul train on. The blood is on our hands.

God has been speaking to me for one year about writing this book. I had a fear of the controversy it would stir up in addition to who would like and dislike me. Like other saints of God, I was allowing compromise to eat me up. As a peculiar believer in Christ you will be persecuted for protecting God's holiness. Don't be afraid of holding on to God's word and being different. God spoke to many believers about going to their leaders, friends, saved family members about the spirit of compromise they have allowed in their churches, homes and lives. It's time to share this book with them and tell them what God has to say about respecting and honoring his temple.

Where and who is God's temple? We are his holy temple. The Holy Spirit lives and abides in us. We should not feel comfortable about being or living ungodly.

Does your temple look like Jesus? Are you a counterfeit? What makes you different from the world? The songs that are played in your church, can you use them for altar call? If unbelievers came to your church could they tell the music being played was gospel, praise or worship vs. the secular songs? Could you play all the songs in your church for Jesus?

Does your church perform dances, hip-hop, stomping or do they minister? What makes your dance moves different from the world's dance moves? Does the unbeliever feel convicted by the dances performed in your church?

Lastly, does your dress wear reflect God's holiness? Is your body exposed? Do you dress like a child of royalty? Is your dress wear to tight? Do you ask Jesus what to wear? If you had to stand before God would he be pleased with your attire? Are your clothes wrinkled? Are your clothes clean? If someone came to your job, families function and asked them do you reflect the character of Christ inwardly and outwardly what would they say?

I Corinthians 6:19-20 'What? Know ye not that your body is the temple of Holy Ghost which is in you, which ye have of God, and ye are not your own? For ye are bought with a price: therefore glorify God in your body, and in your spirit, which are God's.'

As born again believers you no longer belong to yourself but to God. Everything we do with our bodies we will be judged. Is God pleased with you? Jesus is soon to come and pick up his church. He is coming for a church without spot or wrinkle. He is coming for a church that's looking for him. Are you looking for Jesus? Are you pursuing Jesus Christ? Will he be able to recognize you when he comes? Is your hope in him?

I heard a preacher say, 'Believers have the most expensive gift in the cheapest containers. God makes us beautiful inwardly first and then radiant on the outside if we live, walk and talk like him.'

In **Matthew 6:33 it says, 'But seek ye first the kingdom of God, and his righteousness; and all these things shall be added unto you.'**

How simple God makes things. Seek him; please him and he will add all things unto you. I hope God will be able to identify you when he comes back to pick up his church.

WHO'S ANOINTING IS ON YOUR LIFE

Born Again believers who join the church have a responsibility to know who labors among them. A pastor overseeing his flock must have the capability to identify the sheep from the wolves.

In most transactions today people need identification. The purpose of identification is to prove who they are. In order to leave the country you need more than identification you need a passport. A passport is an official document which proves the identity and nationality of the person it was issued to.

Most of the time believers join ministries for the wrong reasons. **Here are ten top reasons not to join a church.**

1) It's a tradition in my family.
2) I'm only here because the Pastor is nice.
3) The church cooks really good food.
4) This ministry gives away free clothes and food every fourth Saturday.
5) My friend attends this ministry.
6) I attend the same church as my boss so I can get a big bonus and raise.
7) My boyfriend is the Assistant Pastor who happens to be married.
8) I can't get enough of that good singing from the choir.
9) I got accepted at this church because I sing high notes, live a low life but the leaders do to. I know I won't be judged.
10) I'm attracted to the First Lady.

Yolanda Gilliam

Can I add one more . . . . ?

***11) The church is close to my house.

People of God have lost their identity. There are many church hoppers. Soon, pastors will have to make it mandatory to check member's spiritual passports. I'm pleading with pastors and leaders to be sure you know where your flock is coming from. You do not want another pastor's left over's. Some members come to your ministry to be you. God did not call them to the seat of a pastor, prophet and nothing else. God wants them to be still and wait for instruction. We are running spiritual foster homes. People go from place to place hiding their sin somewhere else.

Unfortunately, for those who have been hurt by other ministries through unfortunate experiences you have to be careful. Don't rush in a ministry trying to be the spiritual superman or spiritual diva. Stop being offended so quickly. Talk to the Pastor about some problems you were having at another ministry. Allow him time to investigate the situation to be sure you have the right motives for the ministry. Don't be so quick to tell on everybody without telling on yourself. We have made church one big circus. Remember the purpose for being apart of a ministry is to bring souls to Christ. Stop depending on man to be your salvation. Stop expecting the church to do everything for you. What have you come to the ministry for? What gifts talents and abilities do you have to offer?

The bible says to be slow, cautious and use wisdom. Men and Women of God be careful meeting alone with your members or non members of the opposite sex. Every leader or member does not have the same intentions. Use wisdom and move forward with extreme caution. Some say, it doesn't matter what people say. Well let me tell you it does matter to God. We should not allow room or place for the devil to come in and create a spirit of discord. In these last days and times we need to be careful meeting with people alone because people are watching our walk in Christ. It is not our right as Christians to bring discord or assumptions against the kingdom of God. We must be mindful to set a Godly, righteous example.

When a minister is anointed or ordained to pastor over a flock of people, the blessing/anointing on his life falls down on the people the pastor is shepherding. Some pastors are ordained by homosexuals, whoremongers, liars, thieves, home wreckers etc. This anointing is then placed on your life once you join or marry into that ministry.

ALWAYS REMEMBER YOU ARE WHAT YOU PRODUCE!

Some ministries produce those who practice a little righteousness and a whole lot of sin. Some pastors and leaders don't preach about sin because their practicing sin themselves. Living in sin creates a comfort zone for their flock to live and hide in. The pastor doesn't feel threatened that his congregation will leave because they have one thing in common, live Godly some days and unholy other days.

Pastor's do your spiritual homework. Check out your member's spiritual passport. Make sure they are going in the same direction as you. **HEAVEN BOUND**!!!! Pastor's should make a practice of meeting with their leaders often. Pastor's if a leader is over the Sunday school class drop in unannounced to check out what their teaching. Pastor's have a responsibility to check out what's being taught to the flock God has placed them over. Never assume you know check it out!!!

What kind of member are you? Flakey, church hopper, judgmental, encourager, helper, prayer warrior? CHECK YOURSELF!

These are the top ten reasons to join a ministry.

1) Leading of the Holy Spirit.
2) Prayed and Fasted
3) The gifts you have will help build the ministry
4) Help the pastor and wife accomplish the vision God gave them for the ministry
5) Want souls to be saved
6) Desire to tear the kingdom of darkness down
7) Be a financial blessing to the man and woman of God through tithes and offerings
8) Assemble yourself with other believers
9) Need a Shepherd/Overseer over your soul
10) A desire for the word of God to be imparted into your life

Yolanda Gilliam

What have you produced lately? Has your crop survived bad weather? Did the seeds you plant produce life or death?

WATCH WHAT YOU PLANT. THE SEEDS YOU PLANT MAY GROW UP AND LOOK JUST LIKE YOU!

WORDS OF WISDOM

I am so elated to have been graced with your presence throughout this book. I hope it has helped shed light to subjects that have been shoved in the closet for quite sometime. As a believer we want to remember the importance of God first, family and then ministry.

As the body of Christ we do not want to misuse God or each other. Husbands spend quality time with your wife and children. Make sure that your grass is watered thoroughly before trying to water someone else's. Family you are a team of believers working towards one common goal. What is the vision for your family? Don't get caught up with the time taking demons and demonic distractions that lead your family down the spiritual twighlight zone.

Pastors and First Ladies never compromise the word of God. Enforce God's commandments in love and fairness. Be of one mind, in one accord with one another. What you do will reflect on the congregation. Be careful of those who try to steal time away from you and your family. The position that God has blessed you with comes with a great price of sacrifice, endurance and a love for God's people. Some of your congregation will hate on you because of the position you hold. These haters do not want to pay the price you have paid they just want the attention and popular vote. These individuals will suck the very life out of you, attempt to destroy your marriage and children. The bible says watch and pray then do just that. You must protect your anointing. First Ladies be in that office when Sister Snake is in the office with your husband. Pastors allow your wife to speak into your life and use that extra censor God has given her called discernment. Pastors don't allow Brother Smoothie to get all that extra counseling from your wife. Like my momma told me Nip that in the Bud. In other words stop the problem while it's small.

Children be obedient and listen to your mom or dad. Stop having something negative to say. Pray for your parents or whom God has placed in your life. Stop kicking your parent's advice out the door and accepting your friend's advice. Remember most of your friends are not going to give you sound advice. They will tell you things that they want to do instead of what's best for you. Some words of wisdom I don't want to hear but I have Godly mentors in my life that look out for my soul. My mentors want to see me become successful. Sometimes what they say hurts but they give me words of wisdom that line up with the word of God. I am blessed when I'm obedient to my leaders but most of all God. Be careful of grown ups who talk about your parents. These are wolves out to steal your anointing and mess up your life. Most people who are miserable love company. These people will recruit you with words you want to hear, watch you go down and talk about how pitiful you are!!! Unfortunately it may be a leader in your church, a best friend of mom or dad, your siblings spouse, a teacher, t.v. program, or friend. Stay in the word of God, listen to Godly music, communicate with your parents or Godly mentors about anyone who is speaking the opposite of God's word. BE A YOUTH ON FIRE AND SERIOUS ABOUT JESUS!!!!

Leaders, God has placed you in the ministry to help assist the pastor and his wife. Protect your shepherd through prayer and fasting. They need your help. Sometimes as leaders we pray for food and eat it up real fast. That is not fasting and praying. STOP EATING FOR A MINUTE AND PRAY THE WORD OF GOD! Leaders work together not against each other. Stop using your position as a tool to destroy or manipulate. Here is the biggest problem of them all. Stop saying the pastor told you to say it when it's you that's saying it. Don't be a coward!!!! Secondly, when a leader has the opportunity to teach God's word don't use the pulpit to tell people you don't like how you feel about them. Follow what God says and stick to the leading of the Holy Spirit. The majority of ministry workers and members are watching you. Some watch waiting on a mistake so they can use that as an excuse to sin or go back to a worldly lifestyle. Be a leader of prayer, fasting, reader of God's word and fairness. God is depending on you to help build his kingdom not tear it down.

In conclusion, stay prayerful and keep your eyes on Jesus. Stop idol gossiping! Gossiping will keep you financially poor and leave you in bad health. I once heard a pastor say, 'Stop worrying about your neighbor's yard, when you have some weeds you need to throw out of your own yard.'

If we would focus our eyes on the prize we would be in a much better position. I thank God for this time of correction, encouragement and insight of some of the problems that need to be addressed in our churches today. May God continue to use us as vessels to help a lost and dying world? When we accept our Savior Jesus Christ as Lord we no longer belong to ourselves but to Jesus. Become a servant ready to serve. Become humble with a teachable spirit.

We can not be the men and women of God without the help of the Holy Spirit. Our family or spiritual family should never be compromised, misused or mislead. It is our duty and responsibility to keep God as our head, family as our foundation and the ministry as the tool to help unbelievers be saved from their sins through our gifts, talents and abilities.

God bless you!!!

ABOUT THE AUTHOR

Yolanda C. Gilliam was born and raised in Los Angeles, CA. As a young girl she has always had a passion for reading, writing and helping people. Yolanda presently works with Ladybug Ministry a non-profit organization who provides food, clothing and furniture to families. She is also a motivational speaker for young people and continues to teach music with her brother and best friend Carl A. Hairston. As a new author she hopes to address and expose many controversial issues that have been hidden in our churches. Yolanda attends **The Way, The Church** in Los Angeles, CA where **Bishop and First Lady W. A. Garrett** pastor. Yolanda's prayer is that God will continue to use her to minister to his people throughout the world.

If you would like more information about future books to be released or book signing events please write to:

Destiny Changers
5198 Arlington Avenue Ste. 670
Riverside, CA 92504
Attn: Yolanda C. Gilliam